PLANTS AT YOUR FINGERTIPS

PLANTS FOR THE
CONTAINER GARDEN

PETER THURMAN

First published in Great Britain in 1994 by
PAVILION BOOKS LIMITED
26 Upper Ground, London SE1 9PD

Conceived, edited and designed by Russell Ash & Bernard Higton
Picture research by Julia Pashley
Plant consultant Tony Lord

The moral right of the author has been asserted.

A CIP catalogue record for this book is available from the
British Library.

ISBN 1 85793 110 6

Printed and bound in Singapore by Tien Wah Press

2 4 6 8 10 9 7 5 3 1

This book may be ordered by post direct from the publisher.
Please contact the Marketing Department.
But try your bookshop first.

CONTENTS

INTRODUCTION

CONTAINER GARDENING

Some say that there is nothing new in gardening or garden design, just the revamping of established and proven concepts to adapt them to the contemporary scene. Container gardening, or the culture of plants in pots, is no exception. It dates back at least 3,000 years to when the Egyptians decorated their temples with container-grown plants and used containerization (as we do today) as a method of keeping plants alive during transit. The Egyptians imported very many exotic plants by sea from far off lands in this way. The earthenware garden pot has probably been around as long as humans have moulded clay, and in very large numbers following the invention of the potter's wheel. The Greeks and Romans used containers similarly, and grew myrtle, box and bay in clay urns. They knew that this was an effective growing technique, especially where the soil was poor or shallow.

Early gardeners recognized that they had more control over the plant's environment: a plant growing in a pot can more readily have its roots surrounded by good soil or compost that exactly suits its needs. There is also less chance of soil-borne pests or disease becoming a problem. Although regular watering and seasonal feeding are obviously essential, they can be monitored and accurately administered depending on the weather and time of year.

TENDING POTTED LILIES IN A VICTORIAN CONSERVATORY.

TERRACOTTA URNS GRACE A TUSCAN GARDEN.

The Italian Renaissance gardens used containers as an essential design element. Lines of huge terracotta urns filled with lemon and orange trees were placed like sentinels on expansive terraces. Elsewhere, a row would be used to create, enclose or divide two spatial areas of grass. The increased use of plant containers closely follows the development of protected cropping. Today, just as then, plants in containers can be easily moved in and out of some form of shelter as growth and climatic changes dictate. The Italians moved their urns of lemons and oranges into special frost-free houses during the winter months. These were among the first orangeries and others were later to be found in many northern European countries – especially Britain.

Since this period, the culture of plants in pots has gone from strength to strength alongside the development of the greenhouse. The first truly commercial greenhouses in Britain were erected in the 1860s. Plant collecting expeditions were bringing back new exotic species from every corner of the empire. Many were decorative and a few of significant economic importance. The Palm House at Kew was full of economic crops and tropical plants, all grown in containers.

Both the Victorians and the Edwardians loved plants and with conservatories becoming highly fashionable flowering plants and ferns were constantly on the move into the house or garden for an extra splash of colour or foliage interest.

In the early part of this century hardy plants, commercially grown for selling on, were still usually cultivated in the 'field'. Commercial hardy nursery stock growers had acres of shrubs, trees, perennials and other plants that were lifted in the dormant season and offered for sale.

In the USA in the 1930s, methods changed and nursery stock began to be grown in containers – in second-hand food cans, to be precise. This curious development revolutionized the plant growing industry. It meant that plants could be sold and planted-out all year round. It is estimated that in the UK today over 56 million container-grown trees and shrubs are sold in garden centres every year.

In the latter half of this century, the average garden has greatly diminished in size, especially in towns and cities. Some gardeners have room only for a patio, while others make do with just a balcony or even a windowsill. The growth in popularity of container gardening has been inevitable, born, as it was, out of necessity.

CONTAINERS

It is important carefully to select the most appropriate container for your needs. Not only the basic practical considerations such as whether it is big enough for the plant and light enough to move easily, but also the often forgotten or ignored design considerations.

The overall style of a container should be both complementary to and compatible with its proposed setting, be it informal or formal, traditional or contemporary. The colour should harmonize or contrast but not clash with the existing garden tones nearby, the colour of the house, the patio and the colours of the plants you are going to put in it.

The range of materials available to the gardener today is quite daunting, and as a result many people have a tendency to 'mix' but not 'match' containers. This can adversely affect the overall look and feel of a garden, patio or balcony. It is usually better to 'keep it simple' and select one suitable style of container or material type that blends well with the location and the existing garden elements and stick to that alone. Using one or few different styles or patterns, or perhaps a variation on one theme throughout your garden, will also contribute to creating a more unified garden effect.

The style of a container depends on the material it is made of as well as its shape and pattern. Many are based on a known traditional style or historic period, others are totally new, striving to ring the changes and link in with modern architecture or perhaps complement contemporary paving or garden furniture products.

On the practical side there are a number of factors which will determine the right container. Size will naturally depend on the space available, the area of patio or width of window sill for example. It will also be governed by the type of plants you wish to grow. Larger plants such as shrubs or small trees will require a deep pot to accommodate the roots, whereas alpines or annuals will need only 10 or 15 cm.

Strength and mobility should also be considered. All containers should withstand a few knocks but this is especially important with those that are going to be constantly moved around – perhaps in and out of the conservatory with the changing seasons. Mobility is related to weight. It is no good having a pot that needs to be moved about if you can't lift it. It may be practical only to use heavy containers in a permanent siting and at ground level. Conversely, small, light pots prone to blowing over in high winds must not be fragile. Containers vary in durability. All materials are prone to

CONTAINERS ARE IDEAL FOR BALCONY AND ROOF GARDENS.

different degrees to weathering, light degradation and the adverse effects of the continual cycle of wetness and dryness and the associated expansion and contraction of the compost.

They must also be safe – stable and not prone to tipping over as well as inert, thus not reacting with fertilizers, moisture or chemicals. Containers also vary in their porosity and insulation qualities. The more porous the material, the less insulation there is in winter. A porous container will also need more watering.

Lastly there is the question of cost. Containers can vary in price from a few pence for a simple 7 cm diameter plastic pot to literally thousands of pounds for an antique stone or lead urn.

The various types of containers available have different characteristics. All have both good and bad points. There is only one thing that they have in common and that's that they all need to have a drainage hole. Let's look at the basic types more closely:

Stone

These are most commonly made from crushed stone that is then reconstituted by mixing with cement and sometimes other additives. The colour and texture will depend mainly on that of the parent rock, any colouring added and the method of construction. Sand or limestone tends to be a natural buff colour, marble will be white. Dry mixed moulds tend to be rough in texture, those mixed wet will have a smoother finish. Either way they can look authentic and many 'up-market' containers imitating traditional or classic styles are produced in this way. Italian Renaissance patterns are replicated in marble, while in limestone one can find Victorian, Tudor and Georgian style containers.

Although expensive, stone containers are long lasting and frost proof. The inherent weight of stone is often matched by the visual strength of many pieces. Some types are not only heavy but a little delicate – they are easily chipped. On both counts they are best left in one position, at ground level. When choosing them, always check the interior dimensions – being thick-walled they are often smaller than you think.

STEPS FLANKED BY STONE URNS FILLED WITH SUMMER BEDDING.

Those containers made of alkaline rock types such as limestone may affect the compost pH, making it unsuitable for acid-loving plants such as rhododendrons, azaleas and camellias.

Genuine carved stone (not reconstituted) urns are seldom seen. They are no longer made on a large scale and usually come on to the market only at specialist auctions as antique collector's items – usually at extremely high prices.

Concrete

The difference between a reconstituted stone urn and a concrete urn is quite blurred, and is determined by the ratio of the ingredients. Concrete containers are made from cement mixed with sand and/or aggregate in the presence of water to turn the concoction into a fluid that can be poured into a mould. A vast range of shapes and textured finishes are produced – anything from simple concrete 'production-line' quality containers to those made with colourings or a small percentage of powdered stone that get quite close to the 'real thing' at a fraction of the cost.

Concrete containers are tough but heavy. They weather well and are frost proof. Concrete retains heat well and so acts as a buffer against sudden changes in temperature, especially in winter. Like stone containers, those made of concrete are particularly useful for tall, top heavy plants that need a heavy base to prevent blowing over.

They are available in a wide variety of styles and, being mass-produced in large quantities, they are relatively cheap – especially when compared with stone. At the top end of the market the quality is excellent, yet still at a cost most gardeners can afford.

Wood

Wood is a very versatile material for containers, blending easily with most garden settings. Wooden containers range from half or quarter (semi-circular) oak barrels (originally

ORNAMENTAL CABBAGES AND NASTURTIUMS IN A TIMBER TROUGH.

used in the beer, wine and spirit industries but now purpose-built to high quality) to classic styles such as the white-painted Versailles tub which has become familiar from its widespread use outside hotels and bistros.

Half oak barrels are often the cheapest form of large container suitable for trees and shrubs. Those previously used for holding liquor can be picked up at a very reasonable price, but always check that the metal hoops are secure. If they drop out of position all the wood segments can fall apart. This is often seen in retail outlets where stock has been standing out in the sun for a long time. The wood dries out, shrinks and the bands fall down — and are almost impossible to replace. A sound ex-barrel type of wooden container however, can last a very long time. Hardwoods, especially oak and teak are normally used. Shrunken timber can be re-swollen by soaking or filling with water for a week or so (having plugged the drainage hole) and the metal bands can be de-rusted and re-painted or varnished.

Avoid containers made of elm, beech or softwood and those made of non-marine grades of plywood as they are liable to warp or are less durable. To increase the life of a wooden container, treat it with a preservative that is harmless to plants such as those based on copper naphthanate. Avoid creosote at all costs.

The sophisticated styles of wooden tubs, often with a paint finish of white, grey or black can be very expensive. Some modern plastic imitations are cheaper and extremely good and it is difficult to tell the difference.

Terracotta or clay

Earthenware pots have been made all over the world for many centuries. With increased international trade, in Britain today you can buy clay pots of traditional styles from Spain, Thailand, Borneo, Malaya, France, Italy, Greece and many other countries.

Depending on the type of clay, terracotta pots can range in colour from a warm red-brown to a creamy buff. The basic hand-thrown flower-pot is still available at a price, but they have been machine-made for many years. Despite this, they are still attractive and very much in demand. The large Italian Renaissance style terracotta urns up to nearly 1.5 metres in diameter are very popular today but cost hundreds rather than tens of pounds.

Clay pots are either glazed or unglazed. The unglazed type is extremely porous. This means that the clay will absorb moisture from the compost on the inside and lose it through evaporation on the outside. As a result, the compost is well aerated and well-drained, which avoids the danger of over-watering, but although the roots can remain cool, the plants are more prone to drying out. Watering in a clay pot must be more carefully monitored than in other types of containers. You can line the inside with polythene or paint with a silicone-based water repellent to reduce water loss.

An even bigger disadvantage caused by the porosity of clay is the fact that unglazed clay pots, especially thin ones, are prone to frost damage. At freezing temperatures the water

absorbed by the clay freezes, its volume increases thereby forcing clay particles apart resulting in flaking or cracking. Frost damage can be reduced if the pots are raised above the ground and have a reasonable depth of crocks or pebbles to ensure good drainage and air circulation. You can also cover them with polythene in winter to protect them from frost. The thin 'flower-pots' made of clay are most prone to frost damage and are best restricted to a greenhouse or sheltered garden use. The thicker the clay, the less chance there is of damage. A number of manufacturers now guarantee their pots against frost damage.

Plastic
There is a massive range of plastic containers available in all manner of shapes, sizes and colours, made from various polymers such as polypropylene, polystyrene and PVC.

The main advantage of plastic is that it is light and inexpensive. Plastic pots are therefore the best choice where container gardening is above ground level – on a windowsill, roof garden or balcony perhaps, or where larger quantities of pots are needed or where they are constantly on the move. The main drawback of their lightness is that they may blow over in an exposed position.

Brown plastic flower pots have replaced the traditional clay and plastic plant trays have superseded wood for greenhouse and propagation purposes where their ease of cleaning and disinfecting can be a great advantage.

Plastic is non-porous and not a good insulator, so moisture is retained efficiently in the summer – although roots may be 'cooked' during very hot summers – and frost damage to plant roots may occur in the winter. In spring, however, this can be beneficial since the compost is quickly warmed up, encouraging early growth.

Metal
Cast iron, lead and bronze containers are extremely attractive, extremely heavy and extremely expensive. There is just a handful of producers demanding and getting premium prices that are way above most people's budgets. You are more likely to see these types of containers in large gardens open to the public, where they have stood for perhaps hundreds of years.

The hazards of rust and corrosion with cast iron and the problems of toxicity to plants with lead have also contributed to their decline though it is possible to galvanize or seal the metal to prevent any damage. Some plants are very susceptible to zinc poisoning and so will not grow in galvanized containers.

If you are lucky enough to acquire one of these types of containers position it carefully – their character and style demand an important position perhaps as a focal point or centre-piece. Alternatively, look out for second-hand metal objects that are suitable for conversion into pots, such as tin baths, cisterns or old tanks.

Others
Moulded and reinforced glassfibre containers are cheap, light and strong and are used both indoors and outdoors. Fibreglass has been used successfully for reproduction work, to produce Versailles tubs for example, and has the advantage that holes and tears can be easily repaired.

Avoid second-hand asbestos-cement containers – the hazards to health are now clearly established.

Degradable containers made of moulded and compacted fibre are used for propagation purposes and to line hanging baskets or decorative troughs. Some will last up to three years. They are cheap and light but generally ugly and should always be hidden from view.

THE COMPOST

Having selected a container, we must now turn our attention to the compost. As with containers, the range of composts on sale can be quite daunting. It is not worth skimping on the compost. In a container we have the opportunity of maximizing good healthy plant growth. Much of this is dependent on using a decent rooting medium.

For use in containers you need a potting compost. This is a medium, usually containing a number of different substances, which ideally supply optimum conditions for plants. Using the soil from your garden is fraught with problems. Soil types vary greatly and few of them are ideal for plant growth without some form of cultivation or improvement. The soil in your garden may be riddled with pests, diseases or weed seeds. It might lack nutrients or a reasonable amount of air pores. It may also be highly acidic or alkaline, which will reduce the range of plants you can grow.

A manufactured potting compost is a constant, reliable and uniform product designed to be firm enough and dense enough to support the plant and to be moisture retentive and airy enough to supply water and oxygen to the plant roots but still allow excess water to drain away. Nutrients are added in prescribed ratios and quantities based on years of research. When purchased, they are free of weeds, pests and disease. Composts aim to retain all the qualities of a good soil and exclude all bad properties. They can be divided up into loam-based or loamless composts.

Loam-based composts such as John Innes types are made up of sterilized soil, sand, a small amount of peat and, of course, nutrients.

Loamless composts are still mainly peat-based but these are now considered environmentally unfriendly due to the depletion of peat bog habitats. Consequently, manufacturers are now marketing a whole range of new peat-free composts based on by-products of the forestry industry and such materials as coconut fibre (coir).

Both compost types have advantages and disadvantages. It is generally agreed, however, that in containers loam-based composts perform the best, especially for long-term or permanent plantings. For annuals and other short-term plantings the compost is less crucial – even the cheap, short-life compost used in growing bags is worth considering.

Loam-based composts maintain their structure better and are more constant in volume when wet or dry. Other composts tend to shrink badly when dry and are more difficult to re-moisten. This can be a major problem in containers. Loam-based composts are also heavier, even when quite dry, thereby giving a pot more stability and a lower centre of gravity.

John Innes No. 3 compost is the best for containers. It has higher nutrient levels than Nos. 1 and 2 and is designed for mature plants, whereas the other two are for younger plants that need further growing on.

Loamless composts should not be written off entirely. Being lighter, they are better for pot culture on balconies, roof gardens, windowsills and in hanging baskets.

For acid-loving plants choose a lime-free or 'Ericaceous' compost.

Research is constantly being carried out on loamless composts and they are improving with every year. Some have been developed with container gardening specifically in mind. These have wetting agents added to improve their moisture holding capacity and longer lasting fertilizers.

PLANTING A CONTAINER: A STEP BY STEP GUIDE

1. Preparation

Existing or second-hand containers should be cleaned and sterilized with a weak soapy or disinfectant solution.

Soak terracotta pots with water so that they do not absorb too much moisture from the compost to start with. Treat dried-out, shrunken wooden tubs similarly to swell the timber. Carry out any necessary repair work, painting or sealing.

Heavy tubs should be moved to their chosen final position before potting up. Raise up on bricks or legs if required. Make sure the container is stable and level.

To avoid staining of hard-surfaced areas such as a patio, a drip tray or 'saucer' to catch excess water is recommended. Some containers come with these as part of the package. This also gives the compost a chance to draw up some of this drained water in its own time. If the drip tray appears to hold water for a prolonged time, get rid of it by soaking it up with a sponge or mop or ladling it out. It probably means that the compost has absorbed all it can and there is a danger of waterlogging which can cause 'drowning' and ultimately the death of the plants.

Line the inside of porous containers with polythene or similar material to reduce the problem of the compost, and therefore the plant, drying out.

2. Drainage

Drainage is essential, so make holes in the base of the container if there are none. Use a drill set to low speed and on concrete, terracotta, plastic or fibreglass containers use a masonry bit.

The bottom of the container should then be 'crocked'. This involves covering the drainage holes with large stones, broken pieces of earthenware, gravel or similar bulky, coarse materials. Avoid alkaline crocks such as limestone chips for

A SINGLE VARIETY OF VIOLA USED
TO STRIKING EFFECT.

acid-loving plants. The layer of crocks should be deeper (up to 150 mm) in large pots containing plants that prefer a well-drained compost.

3. Potting

This includes potting plants into a new container or re-potting with fresh compost into the same container. It is best carried out in autumn or spring (bedding plants can of course be planted out seasonally).

Cover the crocks with compost to a level that will support the root system of the plant positioned at the right level in the pot. Tease the roots out to prevent girdling, and with established plants do not be afraid to shake off some of the old compost. Position the plant centrally and work more compost around and over the top of the roots. Firm the compost with your fingers or a pot-rammer, but not too vigorously as this can reduce the quantity of air pores and could result in waterlogging.

The level of compost should be at least two centimetres higher than required to allow for settlement. There should be a gap between the rim of the pot and the compost. This acts as a reservoir when watering and prevents the compost being washed out over the top of the pot.

Allow for a final layer of decorative gravel or bark chippings. This reduces the germination of wind-blown seeds and water-loss through evaporation on hot days. It also helps to insulate the plant in winter. Thoroughly water-in the plant.

AFTERCARE

Watering is the single most important job. Never rely on rain which is rarely adequate, especially in the summer. In hot weather, check containers daily, especially shallow ones, established plantings or those in a warm sun-trap. Do not water regularly without monitoring the moisture content of the compost. Over-watering is just as damaging as under-watering. Stick your finger in the compost. If it feels cold it is wet enough. If warm, it is dry and needs water. Terracotta pots can be checked for moisture levels by tapping the side with a stick – but not too hard! If there is a hollow ring to it, it is dry. A dull thud denotes that the compost is moist.

The nutrients incorporated in a compost will be depleted within one season. Quick-growing, hungry plants may even need a top-up by liquid feeding during the growing season. Every following spring apply a top dressing of more fertilizer, preferably a balanced, slow-release, granular type. Long-lived plants may need to be re-potted every four or five years into fresh compost. Alternatively, remove the top five centimetres of compost each spring and replace with fresh.

Avoid under or over-potting. Under-potting into too small a container results in a congested root system that will be prone to drying out and starved of nutrients. Over-potting – placing a relatively small plant into a massive pot – results in a large volume of compost that does not contain any roots. This will remain cold and liable to absorb too much moisture to the point of being waterlogged. This may cause the plant to die, while quick-growing plants may put on too much leaf growth at the expense of flowers and fruits.

Tender plants or containers prone to frost damage can be protected in winter by moving them into a greenhouse or porch or by wrapping in bubble glazing, hessian or perforated polythene or covering them in bracken or straw before moving them to a sheltered position. Regularly check for pests and diseases and deal with them accordingly.

PLANTS DIRECTORY

Virtually any type of plant, except perhaps for really large trees and shrubs, can be planted in containers – as long you select the most suitable type of container, compost and location. The Directory thus represents only a fraction of the huge range of possible plants; almost every bedding plant and many herbaceous perennials and culinary herbs grow well in containers, so only a few are specifically mentioned, but for more suggestions see the Checklists.

Plants are listed in alphabetical order of Latin name followed by the common name, if any. The common name is excluded if it is identical to the Latin name.

The 'fact line' shows, in order:
Size – average height in metres and spread in metres of a mature plant
Soil – tolerances, preferences or special requirements
Site – tolerances, preferences or special requirements

Note: Heights, spread, and growth rate can be reduced in pot culture when compared to ordinary ground planting. This is reflected in the height and spread figures.

ACER PALMATUM JAPANESE MAPLE

The smaller forms of this deciduous tree or shrub, and there are many, are highly suited to pot culture. The hand-like leaves, often deeply divided, are various shades of green, purple or bronze and are often beautifully tinted in autumn before they fall. The weeping or arching varieties are particularly pleasing in a container – especially the oriental glazed terracotta types. They are normally grafted, so be prepared to pay a little more. Those suitable for containers include:

A. p. Dissectum Viride Group – pale green, deeply divided leaves.

A. p. Dissectum Atropurpureum Group – the same but with deep purple foliage.

A. p. 'Oshû-beni' – leaves change from bright red to bronze turning scarlet in autumn.

A. p. 'Red Pygmy' – slow, dwarf with reddish leaves.

1.0 to 3.0 × 1.0 to 2.0   Moist but well-drained, preferably acidic
Sheltered, partial shade

Acer palmatum var. *dissectum*

Agapanthus campanulatus

AGAPANTHUS AFRICAN LILY

Bulbous perennials with linear leaves and terminal heads of blue or white trumpet flowers in late summer or early autumn. The group known as the Headbourne Hybrids contains many good, hardy garden forms or is available as a seedling strain in its own right. Pot cultivation, however, enables one to be more adventurous because some of the tender varieties can thus be protected in winter. *Agapanthus* like being pot-bound and prefer to be kept dry in winter. Those worth trying include:

A. campanulatus – Wedgwood blue flowers (*A. c.* var. *albidus* has white flowers).

A. praecox (and forms) – very large (over 1.0 m) with rich blue flowers.

0.8 × 0.4   Well-drained but fertile   Warm, south facing

ALLIUM ORNAMENTAL ONION

A diverse group of bulbous perennials with erect stems topped by variously coloured blooms, often arranged into perfect globes. Flower colour ranges from lilac, purple and blue through to white, pink and yellow that appear in the late spring or summer. Some of the taller varieties may be prone to wind damage in an exposed container. Buy in autumn as dormant bulbs and plant 150 mm deep. The leaves can look brown and untidy by late spring so it is best to combine them in a tub with other plants.

A. christophii (syn. *A. albopilosum*) – superb metallic pink flowers on a short stem.

A. aflatunense – deep lilac blooms; tall.

A. schoenoprasum – common chives; pretty *and* useful.

0.3 to 1.2 × 0.15 to 0.3   Well-drained, fertile   Full sun

ARGYRANTHEMUM PARIS DAISY OR MARGUERITE

Tender, woody perennials formerly known as a type of chrysanthemum. These plants, quite rightly, are very popular, producing an endless display of variously coloured daisy flowers from May to August. The foliage is also attractive – deeply cut and, on some varieties, silver or grey. During summer, most garden centres stock a good range. They thrive in pots and give a Mediterranean feel to a patio or balcony. Occasionally they are available as quarter or half-standards – at a price. Protect in winter or take cuttings in September. *A. frutescens* is the common species but there are many other varieties, among them *A.* 'Vancouver', a double pink turning to blush.

0.9 × 0.9   Well-drained   Sun

ASTELIA

This is a beautiful evergreen perennial, a member of the lily family, although from its appearance you would scarcely think so. It is available but may need some tracking down. It has no generally accepted common name, but 'Silver Sword' would be appropriate and attempts to describe its main attribute – the leaves – which are silver-grey and shoot up from a tussocky base and gently arch over at the tips. It is supposed to be slightly tender but in my garden it has lasted over six

Argyranthemum 'Vancouver'

years without any winter protection. *A. nervosa* and the variety *A. n.* var. *chathamica* are the types usually offered.

0.6 × 1.0   Well-drained, fertile   Sun or part shade

BETULA BIRCH
The birches are a common and popular group of deciduous trees, most of which get too large for pots, but there are a few which are slow-growing and small enough for consideration in large containers where height for privacy or screening is required:
B. pendula 'Youngii' – Young's Weeping Birch, a small weeping tree suitable for large containers.
B. p. 'Golden Cloud' – a shrubby birch with bright golden-yellow leaves, requiring a sheltered position to look its best.
B. 'Trost's Dwarf' – a true dwarf with light green, thread-like leaves.

3.0 × 2.0 (those listed)   Any compost   Sun or part shade

BUDDLEJA BUTTERFLY BUSH
Most of the buddlejas are too vigorous and bulky for pot culture but they are such attractive deciduous shrubs, with fragrant flower spikes that are loved by butterflies, that it is worth trying some of the smaller varieties, such as:
B. davidii var. *nanhoensis* – a delightful variety of the main

species which is smaller in size and all its parts. The flowers are lilac but there are darker forms including 'Nanho Blue' and 'Nanho Purple'.

B. davidii 'Harlequin' – also more compact, with creamy-white variegated leaves and reddish-purple flowers.

1.5 × 1.5   Well-drained   Sun

CAMELLIA

This is a massive group (over 200 species) of aristocratic evergreen shrubs many of which are suitable for containers. They have dark, glossy green leaves and spectacular flowers which are mainly pink, rose-red or white that can be single, semi-double, double or a cross between these types (Anemone or Peony flowered). *C. japonica* is the common species with literally hundreds of named varieties. A cross between this species and another has produced the other main group *C. × williamsii*. Camellias are woodland plants in the wild, so they appreciate a sheltered site – especially protected from the morning sun which, following a frost, can cause flower-bud drop. In a container the compost must be acidic.

2.0 × 1.5   Acid compost   North or west facing, dappled shade

CHAMAEROPS HUMILIS DWARF FAN PALM

This is one of only two palms native to Europe. It requires warmth and shelter and is ideal for city gardens which have a warmer micro-climate than the surrounding countryside. In rural areas it is best restricted to the south and western regions of Britain. It makes a dense clump of large, fan-shaped, deeply divided leaves that give a tropical effect.

1.5 × 1.0   Fertile compost   Warm, sun or part shade

CHOISYA TERNATA MEXICAN ORANGE BLOSSOM

An evergreen shrub with shiny, dark-green aromatic leaves and in spring through to summer and again in autumn clusters of pure white fragrant flowers. 'Sundance' is a yellow-

Buddleja davidii var. *nanhoensis*
'Nanho Blue'

Camellia japonica 'Coquettii'

Camellia × *williamsii* 'Muskoka'

Chamaerops humilis

Choisya ternata

Citrus fruit

Clematis × durandii

leaved form that requires high light levels to keep its leaf colour.

1.5 × 1.5   Any compost   Sun or shade

CITRUS

Oranges, lemons, limes and grapefruits are classic container plants, enjoying the summer sun outdoors, perhaps on a patio and then moved into a greenhouse or conservatory for the winter. They have attractive evergreen foliage and some produce thorny stems. At least one nursery in Britain special-izes in growing citrus fruits and it is surprising how many varieties fruit freely in our climate.

1.5 × 1.0   Well-drained   South facing wall/conservatory

CLEMATIS

A large and important group of evergreen and deciduous woody or herbaceous climbers or sprawlers. All prefer a cool, moist root run, so in a container they are best positioned in the shade where the stems can reach the sun. A mulch of bark or shingle on the surface of the compost will also help. Some species and forms are too vigorous for pot culture, but there is an impressive range of hybrids that should be cut down hard every spring which will suit (those in the Jackmanii, Texensis and Viticella groups). *C. × durandii, C. heracleifolia and C. × jouiniana* are herbaceous types with sprawling habits that look attractive cascading over the sides of containers.

1.0 to 4.0 × 1.0 to 3.0   Well-drained, cool   Sun or part shade

CONVOLVULUS CNEORUM
This is a very choice member of the bindweed family. It is a slightly tender, compact evergreen sub-shrub with beautiful silver leaves and, in summer, pure white morning glory type flowers are produced which are red in bud. Perfect for containers in a warm, sunny position. *C. sabatius* is a small, sprawling relative with clear blue flowers.

0.4 × 0.4   Well-drained   Sun

CORDYLINE AUSTRALIS CABBAGE TREE
A distinctive shrub or small tree with crowns of evergreen sword-like leaves. The flowers are small, white and fragrant

Convolvulus cneorum

and appear in large panicles in early summer. It is prone to winter cold and the leaves should be gathered up, tied together with string and covered in sacking to reduce the chance of damage. Even if frosting does occur, the roots may remain intact and re-shoot in the spring so do not discard the plant too early. The form 'Albertii' has white, red, and green-striped leaves. 'Sundance' has a red stripe and leaf base. *C. a. purpurea* has purple foliage. The 'Torbay' series which includes 'Torbay Dazzler' has variously coloured leaves that are very attractive but it is more tender. *C. indivisa* has larger leaves but is supposed to be hardier than *C. australis*. *C. kaspar* is probably tender but is described as being the most beautiful of all cordylines with short, fat leaves and is easy to grow in a pot.

2.0 × 1.0   Well-drained   Sun or part shade

CROCUS

Short, easy to grow corms which, between the various species and forms, produce flowers from August through to February. All are good for pot culture perhaps with a deciduous shrub or perennial to give out-of-season colour.

C. vernus – the Dutch crocus, large-flowered and highly bred to the point of garishness.

C. speciosus – pale purple-blue flowers in autumn.

C. tommasinianus – lilac, purple or violet flowers in spring.

0.15 × 0.1   Well-drained   Sun or light shade

ERICA CARNEA HEATHER

This and *Calluna vulgaris* are the most commonly planted species of heather. The flowers appear in winter to brighten up an otherwise colourless patio. There are hundreds of named varieties with miniature bell-like flowers of various hues that are produced all over the dense hummocks of ever-green foliage. Unlike most heathers *E. carnea* tolerates chalk, so in a container it does not require an acidic compost.

0.2 × 0.4   Well-drained   Full sun

Cordyline australis purpurea

Crocus speciosus

Erica carnea 'Myretoun Ruby'

Fuchsia 'Mrs Popple'

FUCHSIA

The showy pendulous flowers of fuchsia can be seen in most gardens during the summer months. Many varieties are tender, easily increased by cuttings and bedded out every spring. It is surprising, however, how many are true woody shrubs which are perfectly hardy and ideal for containers.

F. magellanica – a big, tough species with scarlet and violet flowers.

F. m. var. *molinae* – white-tinged mauve flowers.

F. m. 'Versicolor' – grey-green, rose and cream-tinted foliage.

Other hardy fuchsias include:

'Alice Hoffman' – scarlet and white flowers.

'Lady Thumb' – dwarf, semi-double, red and white.

'Mrs Popple' – scarlet and violet flowers.

'Tom Thumb' – dwarf, rose-scarlet and violet.

0.4 to 1.5 × 0.4 to 1.5   Well-drained   Sun or part shade

Hakonechloa macra 'Aureola'

GLECHOMA HEDERACEA GROUND IVY

An evergreen carpeting or trailing perennial with small, heart-shaped leaves. Despite being fully hardy it is usually treated as a foliage bedding plant for hanging baskets and containers. The variegated form is more commonly seen with white, irregular edging to the leaves. It is still often sold under the generic name *Nepeta*.

0.15 × 0.6   Well-drained but moist   Sun or shade

HAKONECHLOA MACRA ORNAMENTAL GRASS

This is a fantastic, albeit slow, virtually evergreen grass that is ideal for containers. It is usually seen in its yellow-striped form 'Aureola' which makes a dense mass of arching leaves that are tinged red in spring and autumn with cooler temperatures. Perfect for cheering up a dark corner.

0.3 × 0.4   Moist compost   Part shade

HEBE SHRUBBY VERONICA

Evergreen, slightly tender shrubs grown for both their foliage and predominantly white flowers that last from June to autumn. For containers, go for the more compact, dwarfer varieties such as:

H. albicans – very dense rounded shrub with white flowers.

H. 'Margret' – sky-blue flowers, compact habit.

H. 'Marjorie' – very tough, violet and white flowers.

H. pimeleoides 'Quicksilver' – dwarf but spreading with silvery-blue leaves and pale lilac flowers.

H. rakaiensis – compact mound of pale green leaves and white flowers.

H. 'Rosie' – A new form with masses of rosy-pink flower spikes.

0.5 to 1.5 × 0.5 to 1.5   Well-drained   Sheltered sun or light shade

HELIANTHEMUM SUN ROSE

Dwarf, mainly evergreen or grey low-spreading shrubs looking like dwarf versions of Cistus, the Rock Rose, especially when in flower. It is an excellent ground-cover plant that in a container will spill out over the sides. In a garden centre you will usually find them in the alpine plant section. The colour range is wide but hot reds and oranges predominate. Examples to try include:

H. 'Fire Dragon' – flame-orange flowers.

H. 'Annabel' – double, pink flowers.

H. 'Raspberry Ripple' – red, white-edged flowers.

0.3 × 1.0   Well-drained   Sun

HELICHRYSUM PETIOLARE

A tender, woody perennial ideal for all types of containers including window boxes and hanging baskets. The small, rounded, grey-haired leaves combine well with flowering bedding such as pelargoniums, fuchsias, petunias or busy Lizzies which are able to grow through and over the spread-

Hebe rakaiensis

Helichrysum petiolare

Helianthemum 'Henfield Brilliant'

Hosta 'Francis Williams'

ing branches of *Helichrysum*. There are a yellow-leaved ('Limelight') and variegated varieties.

0.3 × 1.0   Well-drained   Sun or part shade

HOSTA   PLANTAIN LILY OR GIBOSHI
Noble perennials much in fashion today. Indeed some gardeners find their bold foliage and lily-like flowers completely irresistible and collect them in the same way that other people collect beer mats or stamps. The arching clumps of leaves which are blue, green, yellow or variegated can be quite small and delicate or, at the other extreme, the shape and size of a dinner plate. Pick a sheltered spot preferably with some shade, although many new forms are tolerant of the sun as long as

the ground is moist. Watch out for slugs and snails which adore them. Try them in tubs combined with lilies and ferns as the celebrated gardener Gertrude Jekyll did.

0.3 to 1.0 × 0.4 to 1.0   Any fertile compost   Shade or some sun

HYDRANGEA

A very variable group of shrubs, small trees and climbers normally represented in gardens by the many forms of *H. macrophylla*, the mop-head or lace-cap hydrangeas. Growing them in a container in a neutral or acidic compost helps control the flower colour. In alkaline soils the blue-flowered forms fade and turn to pink. Choose some of the more compact varieties such as 'Ami Pasquier' (white mop-head), 'Westfalen' (blue-purple mop-head), 'Lanarth White' (white, lace-cap), and 'Veitchii' (blue with white borders, lace-cap). *H. serrata* is a more compact species suitable for smaller tubs. One of its best hybrids is 'Preziosa' with pink flowers that deepen with age to a warm, dark red.

1.0 to 2.0 × 1.0 to 1.5   Neutral/acidic compost   Sun or shade

Hydrangea 'Mme Emile Mouillère'

IMPATIENS Busy Lizzie

Although a tender perennial, the busy Lizzie is usually treated as a summer-flowering annual. Either way it is probably one of the most reliable and versatile plants you can grow. It is the best bedding plant for shade, and in cooler areas in full sun too. Try them in hanging baskets, window boxes, as summer ground cover under trees or as indoor plants where they will flower all-year round. There are various seed strains of mixed and single colours such as Elfin, Super Elfin, Accent and Tempo.

0.3 × 0.3   Well-drained but moist compost   Shade preferred

LAURUS NOBILIS Bay

An evergreen shrub or small tree that can be controlled in size and shape by annual clipping. The handsome dark green leathery leaves are used in cooking, so put one in a pot just outside the kitchen door. The clusters of creamy-yellow flowers appear in May or June.

2.0 × 1.0   Well-drained fertile   Warm sun

LILIUM Lily

The true lilies are majestic, bulbous perennials ideal for growing in containers because most of them need good drainage. Plant them deep (20 cm) surrounded by grit and a good, rich compost. Apart from the various species, there are numerous cultivated hybrids offering a brilliant range of colours. For pots choose from the shorter-growing (about 1.0 m) types such as *L. regale* and *L. lancifolium* (syn. *L. tigrinum*) or any of the Oriental or Asiatic hybrids such as 'Joy' or 'Star Gazer' as well as 'Apollo' or 'Connecticut King'. The flower scent is wonderful, so place the container near a path or on a patio.

1.0 × 0.3   Well-drained   Sun or shade

MAGNOLIA Magnolia

Deciduous or, in a few instances, evergreen trees or shrubs with sumptuous flowers. Some continental nurseries (espe-

Impatiens

Lilium regale

Magnolia stellata

Myrtus communis subsp. *tarentina*

Nandina domestica

Narcissus 'Blarney'

cially Italian) clip them into pyramidal shapes beginning when they are young which makes them suitable for very large pots. The eventual size of most magnolias, however, makes them unsuitable for pots, but there are certain types which, given ample humus, are of a size worthy of consideration:

M. grandiflora – a large evergreen with cream flowers in late summer.

M. stellata – slow and bushy with white, star-like flowers in early spring.

> 2.0 × 1.0   Fertile compost   Cool sun

MYRTUS COMMUNIS MYRTLE

A slightly tender, evergreen shrub with aromatic foliage that has been grown in pots for hundreds of years. The creamy-white flowers appear from May to August. There is a double-flowered variety. ('Flore Pleno') and a small-leaved sub-species (*M. c.* subsp. *tarentina*) as well as variegated-leaved forms. Ideal for a hot sunny patio.

> 1.5 × 1.0   Well-drained   Warm sheltered

NANDINA DOMESTICA SACRED BAMBOO

This curious evergreen shrub looks vaguely like a bamboo, certainly oriental, but in fact is related to *Berberis.* The large compound leaves are tinted purple-red in spring and autumn. The tiny white flowers appear in late summer, followed occasionally by red berries. There are various varieties including one with a variegated leaf. Excellent in a container, perhaps with hostas to give an Oriental feel.

> 1.2 × 0.6   Well-drained   Sun or light shade

NARCISSUS DAFFODIL

The daffodil is without doubt one of the easiest and most reliable of all spring-flowering bulbs. It will grow almost anywhere, including in containers. There are twelve different groups ranging from delicate miniatures to tall varieties with large trumpet-like blooms. As with other spring-flowering bulbs they can be used to give colour early in the year in a tub containing a summer-flowering shrub or perennial. If you liquid feed when in flower you can cut the foliage down as soon as flowering has ceased.

0.15 to 0.60 × 0.15   Well-drained   Sun or light shade

PELARGONIUM GERANIUM

The *Pelargonium* (usually called geranium – its misleading common name) is the most popular of all summer bedding plants – and for good reason too. The flowers can be single or double of various shades of white, pink, red or purple and often speckled and they last from May to September; some have decorative or scented leaves. They are undemanding plants, tolerating periods of dryness and are suitable for all types of containers including hanging baskets and window boxes. They are easily propagated from cuttings taken at any time between spring and autumn and, for the enthusiast, there are hundreds of varieties to collect. Pelargoniums are tender perennials so they need protection in winter in a frost-free greenhouse, conservatory or porch. The main types are:

Zonal – rounded leaves, distinctively marked with a darker zone. Some varieties have very strong leaf colourings (called Fancyleaf Zonals). Upright habit. Often used as a centre-piece in tubs or hanging baskets of bedding (*P. hortorum*).

Regal – rounded leaves with a serrated edge. Larger and bushier than Zonals. Broad, trumpet-shaped flowers usually splashed with a darker tone. Less tolerant of exposed situations and often grown as an indoor or conservatory pot plant (*P. domesticum*).

Ivy-leaved – trailing habit with lobed leaves reminiscent of ivy. Flowers are similar to those of zonals. Ideal for hanging baskets, window boxes or for the edges of containers (*P. peltatum*).

Scented-leaved and species types – a variable group many of which are grown for their foliage which can be grey, hairy,

Pelargonium 'Grand Slam' (Regal)

Pelargonium 'La France' (Ivy-leaved)

Pelargonium 'Lady Plymouth' (Scented-leaved)

and highly aromatic as well as their flowers which can be small and star-like with a delicate charm.

0.4 × 0.3   Well-drained   Sun or light shade.

PHILADELPHUS MOCK ORANGE

Most of the members of this genus of deciduous shrubs are too large for containers, but there are a few compact dwarf types that ought to be considered. They are hardy, easily grown shrubs with mainly white, often highly fragrant flowers in early summer.

P. microphyllus – a small, dense, rounded bush with tiny leaves and flowers that have a pineapple scent.

P. 'Manteau d'Hermine' – compact dwarf with creamy-white double flowers.

P. 'Sybille' – excellent small shrub with pure white, orange-scented flowers that have a pale mauve centre.

1.5 × 1.0   Any compost   Sun or part shade

PHORMIUM NEW ZEALAND FLAX

The evergreen sword-like leaves of this perennial make a striking effect all year round. The strange red flowers are produced on tall black stems but it is the foliage that catches the eye. There are two principal species, *P. tenax* and *P. cookianum*, the former being larger and with more erect

Phormium

Picea pungens 'Globosa'

leaves. There are numerous named varieties and hybrids with purple or variegated foliage.

1.0 to 2.0 × 0.3 to 0.9   Dry compost   Warm sun

PICEA SPRUCE

The spruces are one of the many groups of conifers that not only contain large forest-type trees but also various dwarf or slow-growing forms. These compact types of spruce are suitable for container growing as long as they are not allowed to dry out and are not exposed to drying winds. Over the years, many hundreds of dwarf forms of conifers have been bred – often propagated from 'Witches' Brooms' occurring in the crowns of large 'normal' specimens. *P. abies* is the Norway spruce, our traditional Christmas tree. 'Little Gem, 'Nana', 'Pumila' and 'Pygmaea' are all examples of dwarf, slow-growing forms that differ mainly in their growth habit – conical through to dome shaped. *P. pungens* is the beautiful Colorado spruce which has a number of blue-leaved, dwarf forms such as *P. p.* 'Globosa' and *P. p.* 'Hoopsii'.

0.5 to 1.5 × 0.5 to 1.0   Fertile, preferably acid compost
Shelter and sun

Pieris japonica

Pinus mugo 'Mops'

PIERIS

Highly prized evergreen shrubs with drooping sprays of flower buds often tinged red throughout winter and finally opening in April and May to reveal delicate, mainly white pitcher-shaped blossoms. These provide a complete contrast to the spring flush of foliage which is brightly coloured red, bronze or pink. The new spring growth is prone to damage by late spring frosts, hence the need for shelter and protection from chilling winds. Many are too large for containers but the following are slow and compact enough to be suitable:

P. japonica 'Debutante' – sturdy and low with white flowers on erect panicles.

P. j. 'Grayswood' – very free flowering and bronze young growth.

P. j. 'Little Heath' – small variegated leaves.

P. j. 'Pygmaea' – very slow growing with narrow leaves and sparse flowers.

P. j. 'Variegata' – creamy white variegation flushed pink when young.

2.0 to 1.5 × 1.0 to 1.5   Acid   Sheltered and partial shade

PINUS MUGO MOUNTAIN PINE

An extremely tough dwarf pine from the mountains of central Europe, not especially decorative but suitable for awkward locations where its evergreen foliage will provide structure all year round. Selections like 'Gnom', 'Humpy', and 'Mops' are even dwarfer. 'Winter Gold' has golden foliage through winter.

1.5 × 1.5   Any compost   Any site

PLEIOBLASTUS AURICOMUS

To many gardeners the word bamboo conjures up only a vision of giant, invasive clumps of boring canes and leaves. Nothing could be further from the truth. Many bamboos are dwarf, controllable and have highly decorative foliage. *Pleioblastus auricomus*, for example, is a real gem for tubs: it has purple canes just over 1.0 m tall that form a small neat clump, while the leaves are striped with a rich yellow, especially on the new spring growth after hard cutting back. The botanists keep changing the names of bamboos, and this one may still be listed under *Arundinaria viridistriata*.

1.2 × 0.5   Moist compost   Sun or shade

PRUNUS PLUM, CHERRY, ALMOND

Most plums, cherries and almonds are considered to be trees but it is surprising how many are truly compact shrubs and therefore suitable for tubs. The following are the pick of the best:

P. × *cistena* – the purple-leaved sand cherry, with rich, coppery-purple leaves and good white flowers in spring.

P. incisa 'Kojo-no-mai' – a dwarf form of the Fuji cherry with delicate pinkish-white flowers in early spring before the leaves appear.

P. tenella – the dwarf Russian almond, an upright shrub with bright pink flowers in April; look out for the superb form 'Fire Hill' which has larger, brilliant rose-red flowers.

Beware of *P. triloba* and the pink and white double forms of *P.*

glandulosa. They are common garden-centre plants but, sadly, suffer badly from die-back caused by silver-leaf disease.

1.2 × 1.0   Well-drained, fertile   Sun or part shade

RHODODENDRON

A massive group of noble, evergreen and deciduous shrubs or trees, most of them too large for growing in containers, but those listed below are just a few examples of the many dwarf and compact species that, given the right conditions (and do make sure the compost is kept moist even in winter), are ideal:

R. yakushimanum – a remarkable species with beautiful young foliage in spring and compact trusses of bell-shaped flowers. It is a parent of many hybrids all equally suitable for containers. A very choice, but not difficult plant, worthy of a special position.

R. impeditum – very dwarf, alpine species with tiny leaves and purple-blue flowers.

R. forrestii – slow and prostrate with scarlet flowers.

All of the evergreen or semi-evergreen azaleas are also suitable for containers. Space here does not allow us to do justice to this important group, and to get exactly what you want it is worth doing some serious research. You will find that most garden centres and plant centres stock a good range from which to make your selection.

0.3 to 1.5 × 0.3 to 1.5   Moist acidic compost
Sheltered, partial shade

ROSA ROSE

Roses are surely our favourite flowers and, thankfully, many types will thrive in containers. Roses tend to have deep, sparse root systems so we must restrict our selection to those smaller in stature.

Miniature roses have been around for many years but it is only recently that the range and quality has improved. They

Prunus incisa 'Kojo-no-mai'

Rhododendron

Rosa 'Anna Ford'

grow to just 30 to 45 cm and have tiny, but perfectly formed flowers. There are many to choose from, for example: 'Angela Rippon' (carmine pink), 'Sheri Anne' (orange red) and 'Yellow Sunblaze' (bright yellow).

The next step up in size are the Patio roses – an excellent new group with charming rosette flowers and neat, bushy growth up to 60 cm tall: 'Anna Ford' (orange-red), 'Petit Four' (clear pink) and 'Marlena' (scarlet-crimson).

The Polyantha roses date back to the 1870s. They range in height from 30 cm to 3.0 m bearing many flowers of a wide range of colours. They are mainly scentless but are perpetually in flower: 'Merrouw Nathalie Nypels' (rose-pink), 'Yesterday' (lilac-pink) and 'Yvonne Rabier' (white).

Some of the China roses growing to 1.0 m will also suit containers. They are well shaped twiggy shrubs with a long flowering season: 'Cécile Brunner' (blush-pink) and 'Perle d'Or' (apricot).

Finally, a unique dwarf rose is 'White Pet'. It is seldom without a cluster of its beautiful, dense rosette blooms of creamy-white touched with carmine in bud. Remarkably, it can still be in flower on Christmas Day.

0.3 to 1.0 × 0.5 to 1.0   Well-drained fertile compost   Sun

SALVIA OFFICINALIS SAGE
An aromatic, woody sub-shrub or herb with greyish leaves and violet, purple-pink or white flower spikes from June to August. There are purple and variegated-leaved forms. Ideal for a sunny patio or, for a short while, even a kitchen window box where the leaves are easily cut for cooking purposes.

0.5 × 1.0 Well-drained Sun

SAXIFRAGA SAXIFRAGE
Small rosetted perennials, evergreen or semi-evergreen, usually classed, because of their stature, as alpines or rock garden

Saxifraga oppositifolia

plants. They especially suit shallow troughs or sinks, perhaps with other alpines and dwarf conifers. Add a surface layer of gravel and a few small pieces of rock and you have a garden in miniature. It is a large group, some growing as firm, tight evergreen cushions, others as creeping mats or mossy rosettes.

0.15 × 0.15   Well-drained   Sun or part shade

SPIRAEA

Easily grown deciduous shrubs flowering in spring or summer. Some have coloured foliage. The smaller species and forms do very well in pots, especially *S. japonica* which is a small erect shrub with pink flowers in large flattened heads. 'Gold Mound', 'Golden Dome, and 'Goldflame' are all compact forms with bright orange-yellow new growth in spring and early summer. *S. nipponica* 'Snowmound' is a small mound producing masses of white flowers in early summer.

0.14 to 1.2 × 0.4 to 1.0   Any fertile compost   Sun or part shade

SYRINGA   LILAC

Syringa vulgaris, the common lilac. All its many varieties are too large for containers, but fortunately the genus also contains some beautiful little species, among them:

Syringia meyeri 'Palibin'

Thuja occidentalis 'Rheingold'

Tropaeolum 'Whirlybird'

S. meyeri – a dense bush with small oval leaves and violet-purple flowers in May. 'Palibin' is a charming variety with pale lilac-pink flowers borne in great profusion.

S. microphylla – a twiggy, small leaved shrub with rosy-lilac flowers. It is usually seen in gardens in the form 'Superba' which has improved flowering that is sweetly scented.

1.5 × 1.5   Any compost   Sun

THUJA OCCIDENTALIS AMERICAN ARBOR-VITAE

Another conifer that, over the years has produced a number of dwarf mutations. These are tough evergreens with aromatic leaves that have a pleasant fruity scent when crushed. Examples include:

'Danica' – globular habit, foliage in erect flattened sprays.
'Golden Globe' – rounded habit and golden foliage.
'Rheingold' – very popular, broadly conical conifer with deep, rich foliage.

0.4 to 1.5 × 0.4 to 1.2   Well-drained   Sun

THYMUS THYME

Miniature evergreen shrubs with either a creeping or upright habit. Thymes are a mainstay of the herb garden but many, especially those with coloured leaves, are pretty enough for the decorative garden and containers, among them:

T. × *citriodorus* 'Bertram Anderson' – dwarf carpeter with good bright yellow foliage.
T. × *c.* 'Aureus' – Golden leaved with a lemon scent.
T. × *c.* 'Variegatus' – silver variegated leaves.
T. serpyllum coccineus 'Major' – bright red flowers.

0.1 to 0.4 × 0.3 to 1.0   Well-drained   Sun

TROPAEOLUM NASTURTIUM

Annual and perennial climbers that will trail and cascade over the edge of a tub or hanging basket. All have brightly coloured (red, yellow or orange) flowers throughout summer.

T. Majus – the popular annual which is perfectly hardy and apt to seed itself around. There are a number of seed strains such as the whirlybird series with single or double flowers, in a mixture or in single colours.

T. peregrinum – the Canary creeper, a tender herbaceous climber with bright yellow flowers; usually treated as an annual.

3.0 × 1.0   Any soil   Sun or part shade

....

TULIPA TULIP

Along with daffodils, tulips are the most popular spring bulbs. They are often grown as bedding plants being lifted and stored dry after flowering but planted deep (15-20 cm), many will flower for many years without disturbance – especially some of the species types. There are a number of garden hybrid groups such as the Single Earlys, the Darwins and the Lily-flowered types. Kaufmanniana, Greigii and Fosteriana tulips are good, short-growing cultivars with more delicate flowers and attractive, often mottled or streaked foliage. All will grow and flower well in containers.

0.2 to 0.9 × 0.15 to 0.30   Well-drained   Sun

....

VIOLA VIOLET, PANSY

A large group of beautiful flowers including annuals, biennials and perennials. Most gardeners know the value of the pansy, the many kinds of which will together produce flowers during every month of the year. The newer winter-flowering pansies are superb value, often flowering from autumn through to spring. They can be used in all forms of pots, tubs, baskets and troughs. The perennial sweet violet (*V. odorata*) and the horned violet (*V. cornuta*) form flat clumps of long-lasting flowers that are equally at home in containers.

0.10 to 0.3 × 0.3   Well-drained   Sun or light shade

....

Tulipa greigii 'Red Riding Hood'

Winter-flowering pansy

PLANT CHECKLISTS

....

A FINGERTIP GUIDE TO PLANTS
FOR A CONTAINER GARDEN

PLANTS FOR CONTAINERS IN HOT SUN

The following is a selection of especially tolerant species:

Abutilon★
Achillea Yarrow
Agapanthus African Lily
Allium Ornamental Onion
Aloysia triphylla Lemon-scented Verbena★
Argyranthemum Paris Daisy or Marguerite★
Armeria Thrift
Artemisia Southernwood, Wormwood etc.
Aubrieta
Centranthus ruber Red Valerian
Chamaerops humilis Dwarf Fan Palm
Cistus Rock Rose
Citrus Oranges, Lemons, etc★
Convolvulus cneorum
Cordyline Cabbage Tree
Crocus Crocus
Cytisus Broom
Dianthus Pinks, Carnations
Erysimum Wallflower★
Eschscholzia Californian Poppy★
Euphorbia Spurge

Festuca glauca Blue Fescue
Genista Broom
Hebe Shrubby Veronica
Helianthemum Sun Rose
Helichrysum petiolare★
Iberis Candytuft
Lantana camara★
Laurus nobilis Bay
Lavandula Lavender
Mesembryanthemum Livingstone Daisy★
Myrtus communis Myrtle
Nandina domestica Sacred Bamboo
Narcissus Daffodil
Nepeta × *faassenii* Catmint
Nerine
Origanum Oregano or Marjoram
Osteospermum★
Pelargonium Geranium
Perovskia atriplicifolia Russian Sage
Phlomis fruticosa Jerusalem Sage
Phormium New Zealand Flax
Pinus Pine (dwarf species and forms)
Plumbago auriculata Leadwort★
Punica granatum 'Nana' Dwarf Pomegranate
Rosmarinus Rosemary
Ruta graveolens Rue
Salvia officinalis Common Sage (and others)

A hanging basket of pink and red
Pelargoniums

Santolina Lavender Cotton
Sedum Stonecrop
Sempervivum Houseleek
Stachys byzantina Lamb's Ears
Stipa Ornamental Grass
Teucrium Germander
Thymus Thyme
Tropaeolum majus Nasturtium★
Tulipa Tulip
Yucca spp.
Zauschneria Californian Fuchsia

★Tender or short-lived

PLANTS FOR CONTAINERS IN SHADE

Acer palmatum Japanese Maple
Aquilegia vulgaris Columbine
Astrantia major Masterwort
Bergenia Elephant's Ears
Brunnera macrophylla Perennial
  Forget-me-not
Buxus sempervirens Box
Camellia
Choisya ternata Mexican Orange
  Blossom
Clematis
Convallaria majalis Lily of the
  Valley
Cotoneaster
Cyclamen
Dicentra Bleeding Heart
Dryopteris Fern
Euonymus Spindle bush
Euphorbia amagdaloïdes var. *robbiae*
  Mrs Robb's Bonnet
Fatsia japonica
Geranium Crane's-bill
Glechoma hederacea Ground Ivy
Hakonechloa macra Ornamental
  Grass
Hedera Ivy
Helleborus Christmas or Lenten
  Rose
Hosta Plantain Lily
Hydrangea
Impatiens Busy Lizzie
Lamium maculatum Deadnettle
Leucojum Snowflake
Lilium Lily
Liriope muscari
Myrrhis odorata Sweet Cicely
Pachysandra terminalis
Pieris
Pleioblastus auricomus Bamboo (and
  most others)
Polygonatum Solomon's Seal
Pulmonaria Lungwort
Rhododendron
Sarcococca Christmas Box
Skimmia
Symphytum Comfrey
Vinca Periwinkle

Osteospermum
Pelargonium Geranium
Petunia
Portulaca Sun Plant
Salvia splendens Bedding Salvia
Tagetes Marigold
Verbena
Viola Pansy

GENERAL BEDDING PLANTS AND ANNUALS ESPECIALLY SUITABLE FOR CONTAINERS

Ageratum Floss Flower
Arctotis African Daisy
Argyranthemum Paris Daisy or Marguerite
Begonia semperflorens Bedding Begonia
Bellis perennis Daisy
Calendula officinalis Pot Marigold
Coleus
Dianthus barbatus Sweet William
Erysimum Wallflower
Eschscholzia californica Californian Poppy
Fuchsia
Gazania
Heliotropium peruvianum Heliotrope or Cherry Pie
Iberis Candytuft
Impatiens Busy Lizzie
Lobelia
Lobularia maritima Sweet Alyssum
Matthiola Stock
Mesembryanthemum Livingstone Daisy
Myosotis Forget-me-not
Nicotiana Tobacco Plant
Nigella Love-in-a-mist

CLIMBING PLANTS FOR CONTAINERS

Note: Climbers can present a problem when grown in a container. Once twining up a support or clinging to a wall it is extremely difficult to re-pot them without causing damage. For this reason, the Checklist is restricted to climbers that can be cut down hard or that die down in winter of their own accord (annuals, biennials or herbaceous).

Aconitum hemsleyanum Climbing Monkshood
Clematis (those that can be cut back)
Cobaea scandens Cathedral Bell★
Dicentra scandens Climbing Bleeding Heart
Eccremocarpus Chilean Glory Flower
Humulus Hop
Ipomoea Morning Glory★
Lathyrus Sweet or Everlasting Pea★
Passiflora Passion Flower
Thunbergia alata Black-eyed Susan★
Tropaeolum Nasturtium and Canary Creeper★

★Annual or biennial

SCENTED PLANTS FOR CONTAINERS (AROMATIC FOLIAGE AND PERFUMED FLOWERS)

These are especially attractive near a path, seat or patio.

Aloysia triphylla Lemon-scented Verbena
Artemisia Southernwood, tarragon etc.
Buddleja Butterfly Bush (small forms)
Chamaemelum nobile Roman Camomile
Choisya ternata Mexican Orange Blossom
Cistus Rock Rose
Convallaria majalis Lily of the Valley
Dianthus Pinks, Carnations, Sweet William
Erysimum Wallflower
Foeniculum vulgare Fennel
Heliotropium peruvianum Heliotrope or Cherry Pie
Hesperis matronalis Sweet Rocket
Hosta Plantain Lily
Houttuynia cordata
Hyacinthus Hyacinth
Lathyrus Sweet Pea
Laurus nobilis Bay
Lavandula Lavender
Lilium Lily
Magnolia grandiflora Evergreen Magnolia
Matthiola Stock
Melissa officinalis Lemon Balm
Mentha Mint
Monarda Bergamot
Myrtus communis Myrtle
Narcissus (poeticus types) Daffodil
Nepeta Catmint
Nicotiana Tobacco Plant
Ocimum basilicum Sweet Basil
Oenothera Evening Primrose
Origanum Oregano
Pelargonium Scented-leaved Geraniums
Philadelphus Mock Orange (small types)
Rosa Rose (small types)
Rosemarinus Rosemary
Salvia officinalis Sage
Santolina Lavender Cotton
Sarcococca Christmas Box
Syringa Lilac
Teucrium Germander
Thuja occidentalis (varieties) American Arbor-vitae (dwarf forms of and other species)
Thymus Thyme
Viola odorata Sweet Violet

DWARF/COMPACT SHRUBS SUITABLE FOR QUITE SMALL CONTAINERS

Calluna Heather or Ling
Caryopteris
Convolvulus cneorum
Erica Heather
Euonymus fortunei (and varieties) Evergreen Spindle Bush
Fuchsia
Hebe Shrubby Veronica
Helianthemum Sun Rose
Lavandula Lavender
Nandina domestica Sacred Bamboo
Pernettya mucronata
Phlomis fruticosa Jerusalem Sage
Potentilla Shrubby Potentilla

Rhododendron Evergreen Azalea
Rhododendron yakushimanum (and others)
Rosmarinus Rosemary
Santolina Lavender Cotton
Skimmia
Spiraea japonica and forms
Viburnum davidii

SMALL TRAILING/HANGING PLANTS ESPECIALLY SUITABLE FOR WINDOW BOXES, WALL AND HANGING BASKETS

Bidens ferulifolia
Brachycome Swan River Daisy
Campanula isophylla
Chlorophytum Spider Plant
Convolvulus sabatius
Felicia amelloides Blue Marguerite
Fuchsia (trailing bedding types)
Glechoma hederacea Ground Ivy
Hedera Ivy

Helichrysum petiolare
Impatiens Busy Lizzie
Lamium maculatum Deadnettle
Lobelia
Lotus berthelotii
Lysimachia nummularia Creeping Jenny
Pelargonium peltatum Ivy-leaved Geranium
Plectranthus Swedish Ivy
Portulaca
Scaevola
Thunbergia alata Black-eyed Susan
Tolmiea menziesii Pick-a-back Plant
Tradescantia fluminensis Wandering Jew
Tropaeolum Nasturtium or Canary Creeper

DWARF CONIFERS SUITABLE FOR CONTAINERS

The following species all have good (named) dwarf forms:

Abies koreana Korean Fir
Chamaecyparis obtusa Hinoki Cypress
Chamaecyparis pisifera Sawara Cypress
Chamaecyparis lawsoniana Lawson Cypress
Chamaecyparis thyoides White Cypress
Cryptomeria japonica Japanese Cedar
Juniperus communis Common Juniper
Juniperus chinensis Chinese Juniper
Juniperus horizontalis Creeping Juniper

Juniperus squamata
Juniperus virginiana Pencil Cedar
Juniperus × media Hybrid Juniper
Microbiota decussata
Picea abies Norway Spruce
Picea pungens Colorado Spruce
Pinus heldreichii var. *leucodermis*
  Bosnian Pine
Pinus mugo Mountain Pine
Pinus strobus Weymouth Pine
Pinus sylvestris Scots Pine
Pseudotsuga menziesii Douglas Fir
Thuja occidentalis American
  Arbor-vitae
Thuja orientalis Chinese Arbor-
  vitae
Thuja plicata Western Red Cedar
Thujopsis dolobrata Hiba
Tsuga canadensis Eastern Hemlock

SMALL TREES FOR CONTAINERS

The following species are true
trees or standard-trained shrubs
(not bushy types), small enough
for average sized containers.
Beware of placing them in
exposed positions where, being
top-heavy, they may be unstable.
Some may eventually get too big
although containerization will
slow growth down. Many are
weeping forms:

Acer ginnala Amur Maple
Acer pseudoplatanus
  'Brilliantissimum'
Alnus incana 'Aurea' Yellow-
  twigged Grey Alder
Betula pendula 'Youngii' Young's
  Weeping Birch

Caragana arborescens 'Pendula'
Cornus controversa 'Variegata'
  Dogwood
Cornus mas Cornelian Cherry
Cotoneaster salicifolius 'Pendulus'
  Weeping Cotoneaster
Fagus sylvatica 'Purpurea Pendula'
  Weeping Purple Beech
Laburnum alpinum 'Pendulum'
  Weeping Scotch Laburnum
Malus 'Golden hornet' Crab
  Apple
Malus 'Oekonomierat
  Echtermeyer' Crab Apple
Malus 'Red Jade' Crab Apple
Morus alba 'Pendula' Weeping
  White Mulberry
Prunus 'Cheal's weeping' Cheal's
  Weeping Cherry
Prunus mume 'Pendula' Weeping
  Japanese Apricot
Prunus × subhirtella 'Pendula' (and
  others) Weeping Spring Cherry
Pyrus salicifolia 'Pendula' Weeping
  Willow-leaved Pear
Salix caprea 'Kilmarnock'
  Kilmarnock Willow
Salix purpurea 'Pendula' Weeping
  Purple Osier

PERENNIALS AND BULBS ESPECIALLY SUITABLE FOR CONTAINERS

Achillea Yarrow
Agapanthus African Lily
Ajuga reptans Bugle
Alchemilla mollis Lady's Mantle
Allium Ornamental Onion
Alstroemeria Peruvian Lily
Amaryllis belladonna Belladona Lily

Aquilegia Columbine
Astrantia major Masterwort
Begonia (Tuberous)★
Bergenia Elephant's Ears
Brunnera macrophylla Perennial
  Forget-me-not
Centranthus ruber Red Valerian
Chionodoxa Glory of the Snow
Clematis (herbaceous types)
Colchicum Meadow Saffron
Convallaria majalis Lily of the
  Valley
Crinum × *powellii*★
Crocus
Cyclamen
Dianthus Pinks
Dicentra Bleeding Heart
Euphorbia Spurge
Galanthus Snowdrop
Geranium Crane's-bill
Geum Avens
Helleborus Christmas or Lenten
  Roses

Heuchera Coral Flower
Hosta Plantain Lily
Hyacinthus Hyacinth★
Iris Bulbous Iris
Leucojum Snowflake
Lilium Lily
Liriope
Muscari Grape Hyacinth
Narcissus Daffodil
Nepeta Catmint
Nerine
Oenothera Evening Primrose
Phormium New Zealand Flax
Polygonatum Solomon's Seal
Potentilla Cinquefoil
Primula Primrose
Pulmonaria Lungwort
Puschkinia Striped Squill
Saxifraga Saxifrage
Schizostylis coccinea Kaffir Lily
Scilla Squill
Sedum Stonecrop
Stachys byzantina Lambs' Ears
Tulipa Tulip
Viola Violet

★Tender

ALPINE PLANTS SUITABLE FOR SHALLOW SINKS AND OTHER SMALL CONTAINERS

Acaena
Alyssum saxatile (and others)
Anacyclus pyrethrum var. *depressus*
Antennaria dioica
Arabis Rock cress
Aubrieta
Campanula Bellflower (alpine
  species)
Crepis Hawkweed

Dianthus Alpine Pinks (and
others)
Draba Whitlow Grass (and others)
Dryas octopetala Mountain Avens
Erinus alpinus
Erodium Stork's-bill
Gentiana Gentian
Geranium Crane's-bill (miniature
species)
Hypericum olympicum
Iberis Candytuft
Leontopodium alpinum Edelweiss
Lewisia spp.
Oxalis spp.
Phlox douglasii
Phlox subulata
Primula Primrose (miniature
species)
Pulsatilla vulgaris Pasque Flower
Raoulia Vegetable Sheep
Saponaria Soapwort (alpine
species)
Saxifraga Saxifrage (alpine species)
Sedum Stonecrop (alpine species)
Sempervivum Houseleek
Silene Campion and Catchfly
Soldanella alpina Alpine Snowbell
Waldsteinia

Container Suppliers

Most garden centres, plant centres
and nurseries offer a wide range of
containers and suitable plants, but
the following companies supply
some of the more specialized
containers:

Ann's Garden (terracotta pots),
10 Maunsell Street,
London SW1P 2QL

Capital Garden Products (lead and
fibreglass containers),
Hurst Green, Etchingham,
East Sussex TN19 7QU

Courtyard Pottery (terracotta and
stone containers),
Groundwell Farm, Cricklade,
Swindon, Wiltshire SN2 5AU

Geebro (wood containers),
South Road., Hailsham,
East Sussex, BN27 3DT

Haddonstone (stone containers),
The Forge House, East Haddon,
Northampton NN6 8DB

Renaissance Casting (lead
containers),
19 Cranford Rd., Chapelfields,
Coventry CV5 8JF

Whichford Pottery (handmade
flower-pots),
Whichford, Shipston on Stour,
Warwickshire, CU36 5PG

PICTURE ACKNOWLEDGEMENTS

b–bottom/c–centre/l–left/r–right/t–top
Heather Angel 22;
Chris Beetles Gallery 6;
Bridgeman Art Library/Roy Miles Gallery 5;
Eric Crichton front cover inset, 1, 23, 27(tr, c & b), 28, 31(tl),
35(tl & b), 39, 43(t), 45, 46(r), 49(b), 51, 52, 55(t), 60;
Jerry Harpur front cover background (Whichford Pottery),
9(Burgee), 10 (RHS Wisley), 14 (Sainsbury's Homebase), 19, 58;
Andrew Lawson 29, 31(tr & b), 36, 40(tr & bl), 43(b), 46(l), 49(tr), 57;
S. & O. Mathews 40(tl & br);
Clive Nichols back cover, 12, 21, 32, 37, 44, 62;
Photos Horticultural 25, 27(tl), 35(tr), 49(tl);
Harry Smith Collection 15, 55(b);
Peter Thurman 33.